CITIES OF THE
WORLD

BOSTON

BY DEBORAH KENT

13257

CHILDREN'S PRESS®
A Division of Grolier Publishing
New York London Hong Kong Sydney
Danbury, Connecticut

CONSULTANTS

William M. Fowler, Jr., Ph.D.
Professor, Department of History
Northeastern University, Boston, Massachusetts

Linda Cornwell
Learning Resource Consultant
Indiana Department of Education

Project Editor: Downing Publishing Services
Design Director: Karen Kohn & Associates, Ltd.
Photo Researcher: Jan Izzo

Visit Children's Press on the Internet at:
http://publishing.grolier.com

Library of Congress Cataloging-in-Publication Data
Kent, Deborah.
     Boston / by Deborah Kent.
      p. cm — (Cities of the world)
     Includes bibliographical references and index.
     Summary: Describes the history, culture, daily life, food, people, sports, and points of interest in the capital of Massachusetts, one of the oldest and most historic cities in the United States.
     ISBN 0-516-20591-9 (lib.bdg.)   0-516-26325-0 (pbk.)
     1. Boston (Mass.)—Juvenile literature. I. Title. II. Series: Cities of the world (New York, N.Y.)
F73.33.K46   1998   97-26880
974.4'61—dc21   CIP
                                         AC

TABLE OF CONTENTS

Once a year, on a day in early June—until the summer of 1996—cows appeared on Boston Common. Thousands of schoolchildren descended on the Common for this special occasion. Many of them had never seen live cows before.

The Common is a large, grassy park in the heart of Boston. Traffic streams by along busy city streets. The gilded dome of the Massachusetts State House looms overhead. Parents push strollers, office workers eat picnic lunches, and children run and shout. In this bustling urban scene, cows were totally out of place.

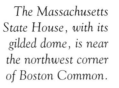

The Massachusetts State House, with its gilded dome, is near the northwest corner of Boston Common.

This sign is at the Park Street Church, next to the Common.

BOSTON COMMON

FOUNDED
1634

CITY OF BOSTON
PARKS AND RECREATION DEPARTMENT

RAYMOND L. FLYNN
MAYOR

LAWRENCE A. DWYER
COMMISSIONER

The cows were brought to Boston Common in honor of National Dairy Week. But their presence celebrated a far older tradition. In 1634, Boston Common was set aside as public grazing land. Any Bostonian, rich or poor, could graze cattle on this site. After more than three centuries, the grazing law has never been officially repealed.

Boston is one of the oldest cities in the United States. Its landmarks recall people and events that shaped the nation's history. Yet Boston is not bound by its past. Its research centers pioneer amazing advances in medicine, computers, and telecommunications.

Its colleges and universities attract students from every continent. In classrooms and laboratories, these young people equip themselves to enter today's changing world.

Boston is a thriving modern city. Its face is turned toward the future.

Yet its history reaches back to the days when Massachusetts was a British colony. Bostonians cherish their city's unique connection with the past. They love their historic houses and their common ground as much as their highways and shopping malls.

Above: Quincy Market, once a meat and produce distribution center, is now a major tourist attraction. Called the Faneuil Hall Marketplace, it is filled with food stalls, retail stores, flower vendors, and restaurants.

*A*nd this is good old Boston,
the home of the bean and
the cod, where the Lowells
talk to the Cabots and the Cabots
talk only to God.

— A toast given at a
Boston dinner party in 1910

BRAHMINS AND BOSSES

Perched on a peninsula between the Charles River and the harbor, Boston has always been a thriving seaport. During the eighteenth and nineteenth centuries, Boston merchants and shipbuilders grew immensely rich. They lived in mansions and sent their children to the finest schools. Families such as the Lowells, the Cabots, the Lodges, and the Saltenstalls came to be known as the "Boston Brahmins." The term "Brahmin" originated in India. It usually refers to the highest class in Indian society. The Boston Brahmins were the city's powerful ruling class.

Passengers on Charles River sailboats have a striking view of the Boston skyline.

The Brahmins were the descendants of English Protestants. Their ancestors came to Massachusetts when it was still a British colony. People of English heritage dominated Boston for some two hundred years. But in the 1840s, a famine in faraway Ireland changed the face of Boston forever. For several years, Ireland's potato crops were destroyed by a fungus called the blight. The potato was the staple food in Ireland. Because of the blight, about 3 million people starved to death or fled the country. Tens of thousands of these refugees flocked to Boston in search of a better life.

Wealthy Boston shipbuilders and merchants lived in mansions (above), while poor Irish immigrants (below) could find work only at menial jobs such as clam digging.

The Brahmins scorned the Irish immigrants. The newcomers were desperately poor. Many of them could not read or write. To make matters worse (from the Brahmin point of view), the Irish were Roman Catholics. The Protestant Brahmins thought that candles, holy water, and statues of the saints were little more than primitive superstitions.

In every way they could, the Brahmins tried to keep the Irish from climbing the social ladder. Some employers even posted signs that read No Irish Need Apply. But eventually, most immigrants found jobs. They worked hard and gained a footing in their new land. Once they became United States citizens, they mastered the art of running for office. They held rallies, delivered speeches, and gathered votes.

In 1884, Hugh O'Brien became the first Irish-American mayor in Boston's history. Another notable Irish mayor, John F. Fitzgerald, was elected in 1905. "Honey Fitz," as he was nick-named, was the grand-father of President John F. Kennedy.

John F. Fitzgerald, elected mayor of Boston in 1905, is shown at left with his daughter Rose, who would one day become the mother of President John F. Kennedy. At right, Mayor Fitzgerald stands with his son Thomas.

The Boss of Bosses

The son of Irish immigrants, James Michael Curley dominated Boston politics from 1920 to 1950. During that time, he served as mayor, congressman, and governor of Massachusetts. Curley never went to college, but he studied on his own. He loved to quote Shakespeare in his speeches. Curley's years in office were tainted with corruption, but he remained popular with Boston voters. In 1943, he was re-elected mayor from a jail cell.

Over the years, Boston had one Irish mayor after another. Bostonians joked that a sign was nailed to the door of the mayor's office. It read Only Irish Need Apply.

The Brahmins refused to accept the Irish-Americans as their social equals. But the Irish had found their way to power. Some of the city's Irish mayors wielded such authority that they were known as "bosses." Though the Brahmins sneered at them, the Irish mayors ran the city.

A CITY OF NEIGHBORHOODS

By the 1890s, the Brahmins and the bosses had to make room for fresh waves of immigrants. Soon, a dozen languages clamored in the streets—Greek, Polish, Yiddish, Italian, Chinese. After World War I, large numbers of African Americans began moving to Boston from the southern states. More recent newcomers include people from Puerto Rico, Haiti, Lebanon, and the Dominican Republic. Boston is a relatively small city. It covers about 48 square miles (124 square kilometers). The city is divided into fourteen sections, or neighborhoods. Many of these neighborhoods are close-knit communities where people share a common heritage and traditions. African Americans are concentrated in and around Roxbury. South Boston, or "Southy," has a distinctly Irish tone. Jamaica Plain has pockets of Haitians and Lebanese.

The North End is one of Boston's most colorful neighborhoods. The fragrance of fresh-baked bread spills from tiny Italian bakeries. On hot days, vendors hawk fruit-flavored ices.

Students making ice cream at the Children's Museum

A Vietnamese girl in her parents' Boston store

Best of all are the lively festivals that draw visitors throughout the year.

Perhaps the most spectacular festival in the North End is the Feast of the Assumption. The feast is dedicated to the Madonna del Soccorso, the patron saint of Sicilian immigrants. Crowds jam the sidewalks, eating, laughing, and dancing. People fling coins to the statue of the Madonna as it passes through the streets on a float. Everyone waits breathlessly for the festival's crowning moment. Harnessed to a pulley, a girl of nine or ten floats above the street. She is dressed as an angel in flowing white robes. The crowd gasps as the angel releases a cloud of white doves from a basket.

A Central American mural in Mozart Park, Jamaica Plain

A musician
celebrating
Chinese New
Year in Boston

Two stone dogs guard
the gateway to
Boston's Chinatown.

Two large stone dogs flank the
arch at the entrance to Boston's
Chinatown. Along Beach Street,
Chinatown's main thoroughfare,
signs are printed in Chinese charac-
ters as well as English letters.
Chinatown overflows with tiny shops
selling spices, souvenirs, and exotic
vegetables. Dozens of restaurants
send forth enticing aromas. The

Beacon Hill (left and above), with its brick sidewalks, cobblestone streets, and lovely old homes, is Boston's most exclusive neighborhood.

restaurants feature delights from many parts of China—cold Szechuan noodles, Mandarin chicken with black mushrooms, and Cantonese egg foo yung. And, naturally, there is plenty of chop suey—Chinese-American style.

Writer Oliver Wendell Holmes once described Beacon Street as the "sunny street that holds the sifted few." Beacon Street marks the border of Boston's most exclusive neighborhood, Beacon Hill. The Hill's stately homes date back to the time when the Brahmins presided over the city. Columned porches, wrought-iron balconies, and fanlight windows recall a world of quiet elegance.

Somehow these homes seem to say that they belong to only the best people in society.

Whatever neighborhood they live in, Bostonians are often on the move. Getting around the city is not always easy. Sometimes it can be a real challenge.

LIVING AND LEARNING

In 1959, a popular song told the sad story of a man called Charley. One day Charley boarded Boston's subway, the MTA (Massachusetts Transit Authority). The system required passengers to pay an extra dime in order to get off the train. Charley didn't have the fare. All across the country, people sang about Charley's plight:

But did he ever return?
No he never returned,
And his fate is still unlearned.
He may ride forever 'neath
the streets of Boston,
He's the man who never returned.

Boston's public transit system is called the "T."

Opened in 1897, Boston's subways were the first in the country. Today, the public transit system, known informally as the "T," embraces a sprawling network of subways, buses, trolleys, and commuter trains. It reaches every corner of the city.

Though mass transit goes nearly everywhere, schedules can be irregular and delays are sometimes long. When they can, Bostonians travel by car. Like cities the world over, Boston is clogged with traffic. Bostonians sometimes quip, "Shall we walk, or do we have time to drive?"

Below: "T" public transit tokens and pins celebrating 100 years of subway service

Above left: The Green Line trolley
Below: Interstate 93 cuts through downtown Boston.

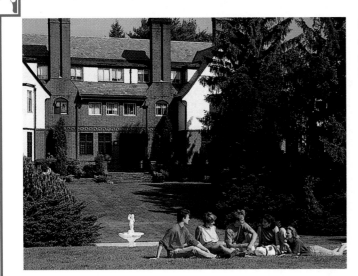

College students gathered on a Boston campus are a common sight in this city of 65 colleges and universities.

A Harvard University banner

Even if you can get around in Boston, you may have trouble finding a place to live. Rents are steep, and apartments are in short supply. One reason for the housing crunch is the heavy demand. Each fall, hordes of college students pour into the city. The influx of students swells the population by about 130,000.

Metropolitan Boston has 65 colleges and universities. Located in nearby Cambridge, Harvard University and the Massachusetts Institute of Technology (MIT) are among the finest institutions of higher learning in the world. Wellesley College in the suburb of Wellesley is one of the country's most prestigious women's

Memorial Church, on the Harvard University Campus, Cambridge

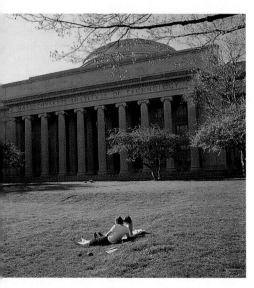

The Rogers Building, on the MIT campus

colleges. Emerson College has a unique program in the field of communications. The New England Conservatory of Music trains performers in the classical repertoire. Students of jazz and other more-modern forms attend the Berklee School of Music.

The concentration of colleges has made Boston a flourishing cultural center. The city teems with libraries, theaters, museums, and concert halls. Mark Twain once said that in New York people judge you by how much money you have, but in Boston you are measured by how much you know. This respect for education is as old as the city itself. It was one of Boston's founding principles.

We must be knit together in this work as one man. We must entertain each other in brotherly affection. We must delight in each other, make others' concerns our own, rejoice together, mourn together, labor and suffer together. For we must consider that we shall be as a city upon a hill. The eyes of all people are upon us.

—John Winthrop to Boston's first Puritan settlers, 1630

PRAYERS AND PROFITS

The first people to live on the site of present-day Boston were Native American hunters, fisher-men, and farmers. They belonged to several small tribes with related languages and customs. The Wampanoags, Massachusetts, and neighboring tribes are often referred to as Algonquians.

John Winthrop and his Puritan followers arrived in Massachusetts Bay in 1630.

In the spring of 1630, eleven English ships reached Massachusetts Bay. The ships carried some 750 men, women, and children. They had been at sea for two long months. Now, they hoped to make their homes in the wilderness along the New England coast. About 150 of these people settled on a peninsula known to the Indians as Shawmut. They renamed the spot Boston, after a town in England.

Most of the new arrivals belonged to a Protestant sect called the Puritans. The Puritans believed that they should live strictly according to Scripture. They wore simple, dark-colored clothes, and frowned on danc-ing and parties. They disapproved of the Church of England, which they thought was too concerned with worldly things. The Puritans felt that prayer and hard work were the keys to salva-tion.

In England, the Puritans were forced to worship in secret. Many were thrown into prison for their beliefs. They hoped to

In September 1630, John Winthrop and about 150 of the original Puritans moved to a peninsula on the Charles River and founded the town of Boston.

escape this persecution by starting a colony in the New World.

The Puritans quickly became successful merchants. Some grew wealthy by shipping dried codfish to markets in England. The fur trade was also profitable. Stylish London gentlemen wore beaver hats. The pelts of American beavers fetched enormous prices in London.

Though the Puritans treasured religious freedom for themselves, they could not tolerate the beliefs of others. They were incensed when a woman named Anne Hutchinson began to preach her own religious views in 1638. Hutchinson and her followers were driven out of Boston. Members of the peace-loving Quaker sect were whipped when they tried to spread their religious ideas. One Quaker preacher, Mary Dyer, was hanged from an elm on Boston Common.

Despite their narrow religious views, the Puritans placed great value on education. Puritan children were taught to read so that they could study the Bible. In 1635, Puritan leaders established the Boston Latin School, the first public school in the British colonies. Harvard College opened in Cambridge the following year. It was named in memory of John Harvard, who willed the school his small but precious collection of books. Today, Boston is home to many of the country's finest colleges and universities. It is sometimes called the education capital of the nation.

Anne Hutchinson, who was put on trial for her religious beliefs and teachings, was banned from Boston.

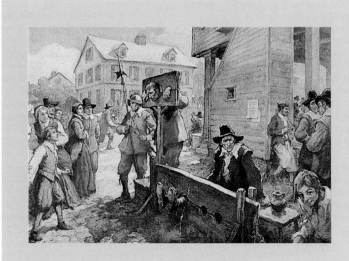

Crime and Punishment

The early Puritans looked on lying, cheating, and refusal to attend church as serious crimes. They found ingenious ways to punish wrongdoers. On Boston Common stood a wooden device called the stocks. Convicted prisoners' arms and legs were clamped into the stocks and held fast. While they sat helplessly, the good people of Boston jeered and threw rotten vegetables.

TAXES, TEA, AND TROUBLE

In 1770, British army tents dotted Boston Common. Red-coated British troops patrolled the streets. Over the previous five years, tensions had mounted between Great Britain and its thirteen North American colonies. Boston had led the colonies in a series of protests against British taxes. Now, the British sought to stem the rising rebellion by taking Boston in hand.

On the chilly night of March 5, 1770, a group of boys began to throw snowballs at a British sentry. Soldiers rushed to his aid. Bostonians poured from their houses to investigate the commotion. Suddenly, the soldiers opened fire on the unarmed crowd. Shots ripped through the street. When the smoke cleared, five colonists lay dead or dying. The first to fall was an African American man named Crispus Attucks. The incident is remembered as the Boston Massacre.

The ill feeling between the colonists and Great Britain was further heightened three years later. In 1773, the British East India Company gained a monopoly to sell tea in the colonies. Bostonians were devoted tea drinkers.

Five colonists were killed during the Boston Massacre.

But they vowed to boycott tea rather than obey unjust British laws. When two British ships prepared to unload tea on a Boston wharf, the colonists determined to act. They planned a peaceful protest known today as the Boston Tea Party.

On the night of December 16, 1773, a band of men dressed as Indians boarded the tea ships. With their tomahawks, the "Indians" hacked open the chests of tea. They dumped the tea overboard into Boston Harbor. No one was hurt. Apart from the tea, no property was damaged.

Left and below: Two views of the Boston Tea Party showing the destruction of British tea by colonists dressed as Indians

Tea crates of the type destroyed during the Boston Tea Party can be seen at the Boston Tea Party Ship & Museum, a replica of one of the British ships boarded by the colonists.

To punish Boston, King George III sent several British regiments to occupy the city. British naval vessels blockaded Boston Harbor. The people of Boston and other Massachusetts towns prepared to resist. They spied on the British troops. They hid stores of muskets and gunpowder. Farmers and tradesmen formed bands of militia, ready to fight if the need arose.

In April 1775, spies in Boston learned of a secret British plan. The British intended to send troops to capture stores of weapons and powder in the town of Concord. They also hoped to seize two Boston rebels, Samuel Adams and John Hancock. The two were staying at a house in the neighboring town of Lexington.

The Midnight Rider

Long before his famous ride, Paul Revere was one of Boston's leading citizens. He was a noted silversmith who made beautiful dishes, bowls, and pitchers. Revere's daring ride was immortalized by poet Henry Wadsworth Longfellow. Generations of schoolchildren have learned the verses that begin,

Listen my children, and you shall hear
Of the midnight ride of Paul Revere.

Near midnight on April 18, two horsemen galloped from Boston. Their names were Williams Dawes and Paul Revere. Their mission was to warn the militia that the British were on the move. The militia met the British soldiers on Lexington Green, at the center of the village. In the ensuing gunfire, eight of the colonists were killed. The British then marched on to Concord and fought another skirmish with the militia.

Today, Massachusetts celebrates April 19 as Patriots' Day. The Battles of Lexington and Concord marked the beginning of the American Revolution. The war severed the ties between the thirteen colonies and the mother country forever.

Left: John Hancock, one of the Boston rebels the British wanted to capture
Below: The militia chasing the British off Concord Bridge in the final skirmish that marked the beginning of the American Revolution

MAKING ROOM FOR EVERYONE

Many of the descendants of the founding fathers were merchants who grew rich and powerful. Much of their wealth came from trade.

In 1831, a Boston journalist named William Lloyd Garrison started *The Liberator,* an antislavery newspaper. Garrison's ideas won him some bitter enemies. Once, a mob hauled him from the platform while he was giving a speech. He was tied up and nearly trampled to death. According to one report, the attack was planned "by gentlmen of property and standing from all parts of the city."

Boston journalist William Lloyd Garrison (right) started an antislavery newspaper called The Liberator *(below).*

Opposite page: In the 1970s, after a bitter struggle, busing was used to achieve integration in Boston's schools.

OUR COUNTRY IS THE WORLD—OUR COUNTRYMEN ARE ALL MANKIND.

BOSTON, MASS., FRIDAY, JUNE 14, 1850.

30

Over the years that followed, antislavery feeling grew stronger in Boston. Some Bostonians argued that all Americans should have equal rights, regardless of race. In 1854, a new law forbade segregation based on race, color, or religion in Boston schools. Another century passed before the U.S. Supreme Court made segregated schools illegal throughout the country. During the twentieth century, Boston underwent radical changes. Factories closed in the city and opened in the surrounding towns. Many families left Boston for the suburbs. Yet new groups of immigrants continued to move into the city. During the late 1960s, Boston was torn by racial tensions. Despite the pioneering 1854 law, Boston's schools were still strictly segregated.

After a bitter struggle, integration arrived at last in the early 1970s.

Like many cities in the United States, Boston is still troubled by subtle forms of racial inequality. Yet it is a city where people of vastly different backgrounds manage to live and work together. Over the centuries, the eyes of the world have often been upon it, as though it were a city on a hill.

Athens was the most splendid city in ancient Greece. It is remembered for its theaters, beautiful buildings, and graceful statues. Its statesmen and philosophers led the world to dazzling new ideas. Its athletes had no rivals on earth. Boston shares many of the qualities of this remarkable ancient city. It is sometimes called the Athens of America.

THE JOY OF COMPETITION

"On this field the Oneida Football Club, Boston, the first organized football club in the United States, played against all comers from 1862 to 1865," reads a plaque on Boston Common. "The Oneida goal was never crossed." Sadly, Boston's National Football League (NFL) team, the New England Patriots, has failed to carry on this winning tradition. The Patriots have competed in only two Super Bowls, in 1986 and 1997. They lost both contests.

Baseball, too, got off to a promising start in Boston. The Boston Red Sox once led the American League. But the team's winning streak ran out with its last World Series victory in 1918. The west wall of Fenway Park, the team's home field, is known as the Green Monster. Sluggers delight in hitting the ball over the monster wall.

The American League's Boston Red Sox last won a World Series in 1918.

Below: Tickets to a Boston Red Sox game at Fenway Park (left)

On the other hand, the Boston Celtics are the winningest team in the history of the National Basketball Association (NBA). Since 1957, the Celtics have won a stunning sixteen NBA championships. Bob Cousy, Bill Russell, John Havlichek, and Larry Bird are Celtic legends. So is Red Auerbach, who coached the team to glory in the 1960s and 1970s. Though the team fell on hard times in the 1990s, fans still remember the glory years. Another Boston sports great is hockey legend Bobby Orr. Playing with the Boston Bruins in the early 1970s, Orr helped bring hockey into the U.S. spotlight.

The Boston Garden was home to the Celtics and the Bruins before it closed in 1996.

Boston's college students score big on IQ tests, but not on the playing fields. Harvard's crew team is the exception to prove the rule. Harvard rowers are masters of strength, speed, and precision. Rowing on the Charles River is a popular amateur sport. Hundreds of rowing teams delight in the Head of the Charles Regatta, held each year on a Sunday in October. There is no prize money, and nobody seems to care who wins. But boat lovers flock to Boston from all over the world to dip their oars in the Charles.

Right and below: Participants in the annual Head of the Charles Regatta

Each year on Patriots' Day, some 10,000 men and women gather behind the starting line for the B.A.A. Boston Marathon. Crowds cheer as they race along the 26-mile (42-km) course. First run in 1897, the Boston Marathon is the granddaddy of all similar competitions. One marathoner, John A. Kelley, entered 61 times (he completed 58 of them). He ran for the last time when he was eighty-four years old.

1983

BAGGAGE TAG
TIE TAG TO YOUR BAGGAGE
CLAIM BAG AFTER RACE

CITGO

CITGO

1983

1983

100TH BOSTON MARATHON®

BOSTON ATHLETIC ASSOCIATION

100th Boston Marathon

1996

DO NOT DETACH THIS TAG FROM THE COMPETITOR'S NUMBER
This tab and label are indispensable for your official recording.

DO NOT DETACH THIS TAG FROM THE COMPETITOR'S NUMBER

1983

DO NOT PIN

THIS HOLE

DO NOT PIN

THIS HOLE

N⁰ 01983

9601983

Bib worn by runner number 1983 in the 100th Boston Marathon

John Kelley crossing the finish line during one of the 58 marathons he completed

THE SOUND OF MUSIC

On warm summer days, jugglers, magicians, and break dancers entertain the wandering crowds on Boston Common. Here and there, aspiring musicians practice before an audience. Stroll along the park's winding paths and you may hear a young violinist from the New England Conservatory. A steel band strikes up beneath the trees. A guitarist perches on a wall, trying out the new song he just composed that morning.

For more formal entertainment, music lovers can go to Symphony Hall. The Boston Symphony Orchestra has been part of the cultural scene since 1881. Though tickets are expensive, there are never enough to meet the demand. Some families hand down season tickets to the symphony the way they pass on their fine china.

A juggler (far right) and a young flutist (right) were among the many entertainers who attracted crowds on one warm summer day on Boston Common.

Students at the Berklee School of Music (left) study jazz rather than classical music.

If you don't like Mozart and Beethoven, you can still enjoy orchestra concerts in Boston. Every summer, the Boston Pops orchestra delights audiences with its lively renditions of familiar melodies. The Pops programs come from opera, stage, and such modern greats as Elvis and the Beatles. Purists claim that the orchestra is a disgrace to serious music. But that doesn't stop Bostonians from packing the Pops concerts.

The Boston Pops rose to fame under the baton of Arthur Fiedler. Fiedler conducted the orchestra for nearly fifty years, from 1930 until 1979. He believed that music should be for everyone, rich and poor. To this day, the Boston Pops plays a series of free outdoor concerts every summer at Hatch Band Shell on the Charles River.

A Boston Pops concert at MIT

THINGS OF BEAUTY

To the Boston Brahmins, art was both a pleasure and an investment. They filled their homes with priceless paintings and statues. Over the years, many of these works have been donated to Boston's art museums. Today, Boston's museums offer a visual feast that can be savored by everyone.

The Boston Atheneum occupies a lovely Italian-style building on Beacon Street. Founded in 1807, the Atheneum was the first museum in Boston to open its doors to the public. Its galleries display fine examples of American and European art. On the fifth floor is a collection of rare books that once belonged to George Washington.

Among the treasures at Boston's Museum of Fine Arts is a portrait of Paul Revere by American master John Singleton Copley. Silver pitchers and dishes made by Revere himself are also on exhibit. The museum has a splendid collection of Egyptian carvings, Japanese brush paintings, and other works from around the world.

This portrait of Paul Revere by John Singleton Copley (above) is one of the treasures in Boston's Museum of Fine Arts (below).

In 1990, thieves disguised as security guards carried off thirteen prized paintings from the Isabella Stewart Gardner Museum. Bostonians were outraged. The Gardner Museum holds a special place in the city's heart, and the theft touched thousands of people.

The Gardner Museum is housed in a Renaissance villa that was transported brick by brick from Venice, Italy. Its galleries overflow with paintings, sculptures, tapestries, and elegant furniture. One of the museum's most beloved features is the courtyard garden with its splashing fountain. During the summer, the garden is the setting for charming concerts of early music.

Not all of Boston's artworks are in museums. The city's monuments and buildings express an artistic vision on a grand scale. A tour of the city offers views of the old and the new, the charming and the magnificent.

The interior courtyard garden is one of the Isabella Stewart Gardner Museum's most charming features.

The Lady with the Lion

Isabella Stewart Gardner loved to shock the proper society ladies of Boston. She once attracted an astonished crowd by walking a pet lion on a leash. On New Year's Day 1903, Gardner opened her home as a public art museum. The Boston Symphony played for the reception, and the guests dined on doughnuts and champagne. According to Mrs. Gardner's will, none of the exhibits must ever be changed.

The old rhyme about Boston calls it "the home of the bean and the cod." Sweetened with molasses, Boston baked beans are a local tradition. The dish was once so popular that Boston earned the nickname "Bean Town." Like a favorite recipe, Boston is a rich blend of flavors. In delicious ways, it combines the familiar with the surprising.

OUT ON THE EDGE

"Pahk the cah in Hahvahd Yahd!" Visitors love to chant this phrase in imitation of the famous Boston accent. Bostonians tend to drop their rs. The word "corner" is pronounced "cawna," and a car becomes a "cah." "Hahvahd Yahd," or Harvard Yard, is really in Cambridge across the Charles River from Boston. About 25 percent of Cambridge's inhabitants are students at Harvard, MIT, and other colleges. It is awesome to think of the brilliant men and women who have walked these streets.

The gates to Harvard Yard, the center of Harvard University's campus in Cambridge

Beautiful blown glass flowers are exhibited at the Botanical Museum.

The Harvard campus boasts nine fine museums, all of them open to the public. The Fogg Museum of Art houses a splendid collection of paintings by such figures as Rembrandt, Matisse, and Monet. Asian and Islamic art are featured at the Sackler Gallery. The Peabody Museum of Archaeology and Ethnography contains displays on the native peoples of North America. The glass flower exhibit at the Botanical Museum is truly breathtaking. More than 800 flower species are rendered in blown glass, each in minute detail. The flowers were made in Germany between 1877 and 1936.

Smoots and an Ear

Painted on the pavement near the end of the MIT Bridge are the mysterious words: "364.4 Smoots Plus One Ear." In 1958, an MIT fraternity pledge named Oliver Smoot was ordered to measure the bridge, using his own body as a yardstick. His measurement still stands.

The home of poet Henry Wadsworth Longfellow on the Harvard campus is now a National Historic Site.

Another Cambridge highlight is poet Henry Wadsworth Longfellow's home. For 45 years, Longfellow lived in this house and walked in the surrounding gardens. George Washington lived here for nine months during the American Revolution.

"Old Ironsides," officially known as the USS *Constitution*, has its permanent berth at a pier in Charlestown. The ship served in the War of 1812. Its nickname is misleading. Old Ironsides is not a metal ship. It was built of live oak, an exceptionally hard wood from Georgia. In battle, cannonballs bounced off the hull as though it were made of iron.

Not far from the battleship stands the Bunker Hill Monument, a graceful granite obelisk. While they pant up the monument's 294 stairs, visitors can think of the British and colonial soldiers who died at the Battle of Bunker Hill.

Above: The Bunker Hill Monument
Right: The USS Constitution, *berthed in Charlestown, a suburb of Boston*

A monument of a different kind stands in the town of Brookline. It is the John F. Kennedy National Historic Site, the birthplace of the U.S. president. A modernistic building in Dorchester houses the John F. Kennedy Museum and Library. The museum's audiovisual displays present some of Kennedy's most stirring speeches.

About thirty tiny islands are sprinkled across Boston Harbor. Over the centuries, the islands have contained forts, hospitals, and poorhouses. Today, nearly all of them are protected as the Boston Harbor Islands State Park. The park's headquarters occupies Fort Warren, which served as a

prison in the Civil War. In the shadow of downtown Boston, the park offers a glimpse of the natural world. Birds nest along rocky trails. Fish leap along the shore, waiting to be caught.

This young tourist seems fascinated by a demonstration at Bunker Hill Monument.

NORTH, SOUTH, EAST, WEST

Like most Americans, Bostonians usually shop in malls and supermarkets. But on weekends, the people of Boston's North End wheel their shopping carts to Haymarket. Women and men at Haymarket sell fruits and vegetables from outdoor stalls. Vendors walk the streets, calling out their wares in English and Italian. They sell candies, pastries, and fruit-flavored ices—the perfect treat for a broiling summer day. A walk through Haymarket is like a trip to an Italian village. Embedded in the sidewalks are brass replicas of melon rinds, orange peels, fishheads, and wrinkled newspapers. They are a sculptor's impressions of what remains when the market shuts down at night.

Another attraction of the North End is Paul Revere's House. Under this roof, Revere raised a lively family of sixteen children. Many of Revere's silver pieces are on display, as well as a huge bronze bell weighing 931 pounds (422 kilograms). Revere was one of the leading bell makers of his time.

A lantern shining in the steeple of the Old North Church was a signal to Paul Revere that the British were coming by land.

Before he made his famous ride, Paul Revere saw a signal lantern shining in the steeple of the Old North Church. Today, the church is a landmark of the North End. Several of its pews have bronze plates inscribed with the names of early Boston families.

The South End is a neighborhood of three- and four-story rowhouses. The South End was laid out around several grassy parks known as squares. Each has a splashing fountain at its center. The houses around Chester Square were once among the most fashionable in the city.

The Old North Church (above and below) is a landmark of Boston's North End.

Writer Nathaniel Hawthorne once said that Boston's waterfront was "devoted to the ponderous, ill-smelling, inelegant necessaries of life." Today, much of the waterfront is devoted to pleasure for the whole family. Seafood restaurants feature clams, crabs, and—naturally—the famous Boston scrod. Scrod is simply another name for a young codfish.

No walk along the waterfront is complete without a visit to the New England Aquarium. Seals bark a greeting from a pool near the entrance. Inside, life on a coral reef is recreated in a giant tank. Pressed to the glass, visitors watch turtles, sharks, and moray eels going about their business.

A bronze sculpture called Dolphins of the Sea *stands in a water basin outside the New England Aquarium.*

Visitors to the Beaver II *(bottom) may throw wooden tea chests over the rail of the boat just as the colonists did during the Boston Tea Party (left).*

History comes to life at the *Beaver II*, a small sailing vessel tied up in Boston Harbor. The original *Beaver* was one of the British ships that brought their unwelcome cargo of tea in 1773. Visitors to the *Beaver II* are invited to hold their own Boston Tea Party by tossing wooden tea chests over the rail. Today's chests are attached to chains. The *Beaver II*'s

crew pulls them back on board for the next batch of tourists.

Along Boston's western edge stretches a green park called the Esplanade. The Esplanade overlooks the Charles River. From the grassy bank, you can watch motor launches, sailboats, and perhaps even a light scull rowed by a couple of Harvard students.

On warm days, the park is alive with joggers, dogs, skateboarders, and peaceful citizens soaking up the sun.

From the western end of the Esplanade, the Massachusetts Avenue Bridge reaches across the river to Cambridge. Often called the MIT Bridge, it offers a splendid view of Back Bay and Beacon Hill, the very heart of Boston.

THE HEART OF THE CITY

One day in 1857, a crew of sweating workers dumped a load of gravel into Boston's Back Bay. The stones disappeared beneath the water without a trace. But the gravel kept coming, load after load for the next thirty years. Gradually, the pile of stones and debris rose above the surface. It grew into a tract of new land covering some 450 acres (182 hectares). This immense landfill is one of the most elegant sections of Boston. Back Bay was designed with wide, straight boulevards and spacious parks. Many of its Victorian homes have been turned into apartment buildings. Some, such as the Gibson House and the Honeywell Mansion, are open as museums. Their polished furniture, carved mantelpieces, and silver candelabras hint at an era of luxury.

The elegant homes and apartment buildings of Boston's Back Bay are framed by the downtown skyline.

Back Bay has its modern side, too. Completed in the 1960s, the Prudential Center is a sprawling complex of shops and office buildings. The John Hancock Tower is covered with sheets of glass that mirror the surrounding streets. At 790 feet (241 meters) it is the tallest building in Boston. Soon after the tower was finished in 1976, several glass panels tore loose in a high wind and shattered on the pavement.

Originally, Boston was built on three steep hills. Two of them were nearly leveled to provide the landfill that created Back Bay. Only Beacon Hill remains. Beacon Hill is a National Historic Landmark. This designation ensures that the appearance of its streets and buildings will never be changed. Apart from the traffic congestion, Beacon Hill looks much as it did in the late 1800s.

Trinity Church on Copley Square, built in the late 1800s, is reflected in the modern glass panels of the John Hancock Tower, built in the 1970s.

Summer visitors enjoy a relaxing swan boat ride on the lagoon in the Public Garden across the street from Boston Common.

The north slope of Beacon Hill is popular with students, artists, and others on a limited budget. In the years before the Civil War, many free African Americans made their homes there. From this base, they fought to overthrow slavery. Several buildings in this neighborhood are attractions on Boston's Black Heritage Trail. Some, such as the Lewis and Harriet Hayden House, were once stops for runaway slaves on the Underground Railroad. When poet Robert Lowell was growing up, his family moved from the south slope of Beacon Hill to Revere Street on the north slope. His mother was aghast. She swore they had moved to the "outer rim of the hub of decency." To Boston Brahmins like the Lowells, the south slope of the hill was the only

The gilded dome of the Massachusetts State House overlooks the fountain in Boston Common.

civilized spot on earth. From Chestnut, Mount Vernon, and Beacon Streets, their stately houses still cast their haughty gaze upon the world.

Across the street from Boston Common is the Public Garden. Its paths wander among trees and flowerbeds. The garden's centerpiece is the lagoon, where swan-shaped boats glide in figure eights. A ride on a swan boat is a must for every Boston visitor.

On any warm day, Boston Common swarms with people. Children jump rope and play tag while grown-ups read or talk. Overlooking the scene is the gilded dome of the Massachusetts State House. Since 1798, it has been a symbol of Boston, this city of change and tradition.

Suddenly, a speaker springs to a wooden box. Shouting and waving, he warns the passersby that society is about to collapse. He is free to state his opinions. This is common ground, open to all.

A young girl on Boston Common tries out stilts during a summer festival.

FAMOUS LANDMARKS

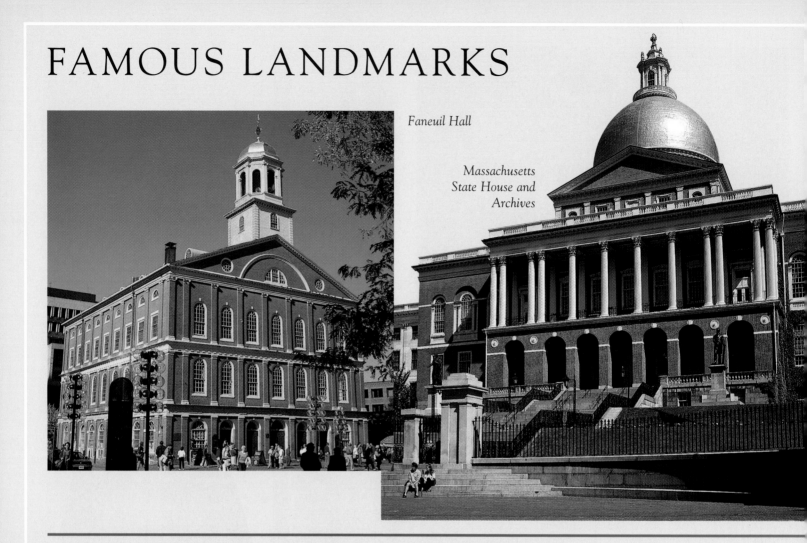

Faneuil Hall

Massachusetts State House and Archives

Boston Common
The oldest public park in the United States. Covering 50 acres (20 ha), the Common is like the city's backyard. It contains an athletic field and a monument to Union soldiers killed in the Civil War.

Public Garden
A landscaped park with carefully tended flowerbeds. Opened in 1859, the garden is best known for its beautiful lagoon on which the famous swan boats operate.

Boston Atheneum
Boston's oldest art museum, founded in 1807. Among the Atheneum's featured exhibits is a collection of George Washington's books.

Museum of Fine Arts
Art museum noted for its French Impressionist paintings. Other exhibits feature Asian and Islamic art.

Isabella Stewart Gardner Museum
Art museum housed in a Renaissance Italian villa. Concerts are held in the lovely courtyard garden.

Massachusetts General Hospital
One of the most important medical research centers in the world. In 1846, doctors here pioneered the use of ether in surgery.

Haymarket
Colorful open-air market in Boston's North End. Bronze sculptures set into the pavement represent fishheads, melon rinds, and other market leavings.

Government Center
Modern complex of government office buildings. Government Center was created in 1962 as part of a vast urban renewal project. It includes City Hall and the John F. Kennedy Federal Building.

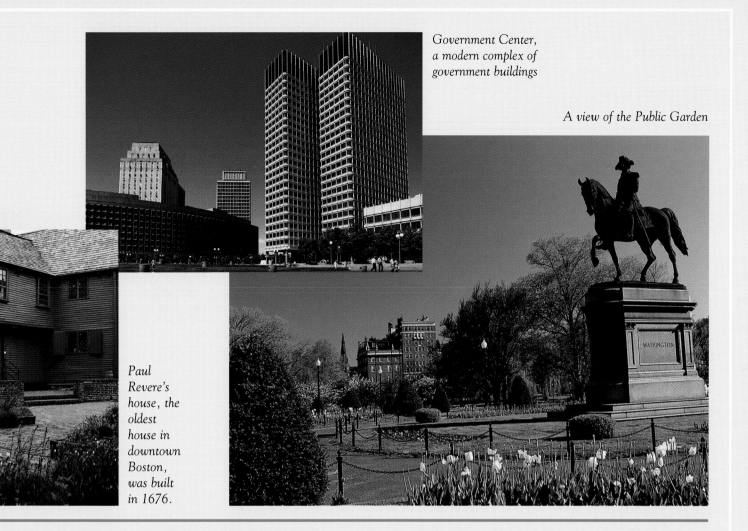

Government Center, a modern complex of government buildings

A view of the Public Garden

Paul Revere's house, the oldest house in downtown Boston, was built in 1676.

Freedom Trail

A series of sixteen historic sites and landmarks, most of them linked by a path of red bricks set into the pavement. The trail begins at Boston Common and ends at the USS *Constitution* in Charlestown. The following are some of the Freedom Trail's highlights:

Massachusetts State House

Seat of Massachusetts state government. The domed building was completed in 1798 by the renowned architect Charles Bulfinch. On the wall of the House chamber hangs the wooden sculpture of a codfish. It honors the fish that was a source of wealth for many Boston Brahmins.

Old Granary Burying Ground

Cemetery opened in 1660. It contains the graves of Samuel Adams, Paul Revere, the colonists killed in the Boston Massacre, and Elizabeth Goose, creator of the famous Mother Goose nursery rhymes.

Park Street Church

Church dating to 1810. In 1829, William Lloyd Garrison preached an antislavery sermon from its pulpit, launching the abolition movement in Boston.

Faneuil Hall

Popular meeting-place for colonial patriots before the American Revolution. It has sometimes been called the Cradle of Liberty. Today, the original hall adjoins Quincy Market, an extensive complex of shops and restaurants.

Paul Revere's House

Oldest house in downtown Boston, built in 1676. It is a two-story frame house where Revere lived with his sixteen children. On display are many of Revere's silver pieces, as well as a 931-pound (422-kg) bronze bell.

Old Ironsides

Ship officially known as the USS *Constitution*. This wooden vessel was launched in 1797 and served in the War of 1812.

FAST FACTS

POPULATION

City:	574,283
Metropolitan Area:	3,227,707

AREA

51 square miles
(134 km^2)

LOCATION

Boston is located in eastern Massachusetts. It occupies a peninsula between the Charles River to the west and the Atlantic coast to the east.

CLIMATE

Boston lies in the Temperate Zone, with cold, snowy winters and hot, humid summers. January temperatures average 28 degrees Fahrenheit (minus 2° Celsius). The average temperature in July is 72 degrees Fahrenheit (22° Celsius).

ECONOMY

Manufacturing accounts for about 25 percent of the jobs in the Greater Boston area. However, few factories are located in Boston itself. Lynn, Waltham, and other nearby towns produce machinery, medical supplies, processed foods, and electronic equipment. Most people in Boston work in service jobs. They are involved in education, publishing, research, and health care. Boston is the leading financial center in New England, with a stock exchange and more than 100 banks. It is also the region's major center for transportation. Cargo ships sail in and out of Boston Harbor every day. Boston's Logan Airport serves about 20 million passengers every year.

CHRONOLOGY

1630
John Winthrop and his Puritan followers found Boston on Massachusetts Bay.

1634
Boston Common is set aside as public grazing land.

1636
Harvard College is founded.

1770
British soldiers kill five colonists in the Boston Massacre.

1773
Colonists hold the Boston Tea Party, destroying chests of tea to protest the British East India Company's monopoly.

1775
Paul Revere and William Dawes ride from Boston to warn colonial militia of British troop movements; British and colonial soldiers clash in the Battles of Lexington and Concord.

1798
Architect Charles Bulfinch completes the Massachusetts State House.

1831
William Lloyd Garrison publishes *The Liberator*, an antislavery newspaper.

1845
Because of the Great Potato Famine, thousands of starving immigrants from Ireland begin to arrive in Boston.

A girl enjoying Fourth of July festivities in Boston

1854
A Boston law forbids segregation in the public schools based on race or religion.

1884
Hugh O'Brien becomes Boston's first Irish-American mayor.

1857
Boston launches a major landfill project to create the Back Bay.

1881
The Boston Symphony Orchestra is founded.

1897
Boston opens the first subway system in the United States.

1918
The Boston Red Sox win the World Series.

1951
Several historic landmarks are linked by a red brick pathway to create the Freedom Trail.

1957
The Boston Redevelopment Authority begins a vast urban renewal project that transforms 11 percent of the city; the Boston Celtics win their first NBA Championship.

1976
Work is completed on the John Hancock Tower, the tallest building in Boston.

1990
Thieves steal thirteen valuable paintings from the Isabella Stewart Gardner Museum.

BOSTON

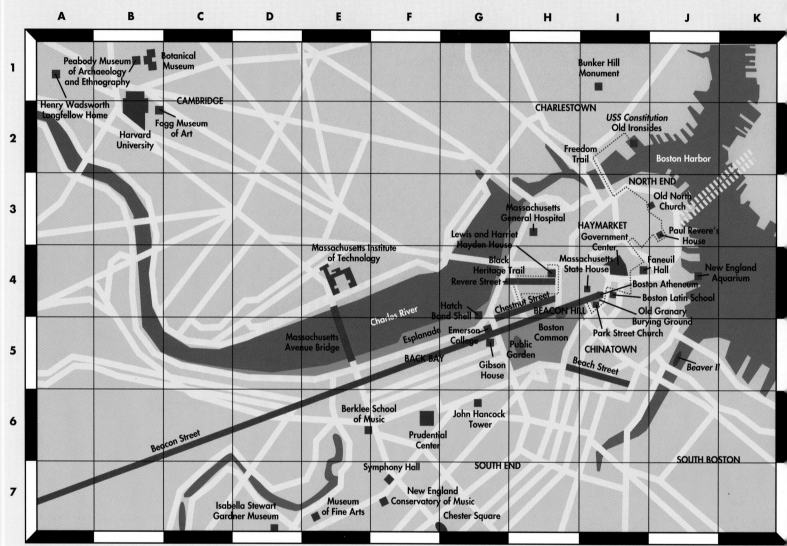

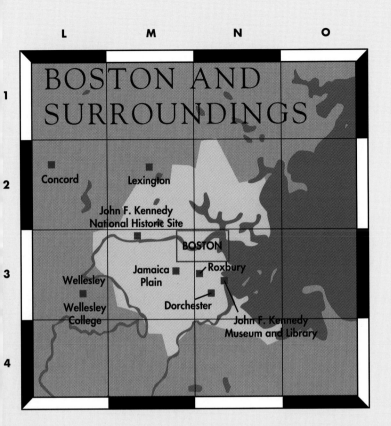

BOSTON AND SURROUNDINGS

L   M   N   O

1

2 Concord   Lexington

John F. Kennedy
National Historic Site

BOSTON

3 Wellesley   Jamaica Plain   Roxbury

Wellesley College   Dorchester

John F. Kennedy
Museum and Library

4

GLOSSARY

boycott: To lodge a protest by refusing to buy a product

Brahmin: A member of a high social class

character: A written symbol that represents a word or syllable

debris: Trash

entice: Lure

exotic: Foreign

gilded: Covered with thin sheets of gold

obelisk: Tall, tapered 4-sided stone pillar with a pyramid-shaped cap

quip: To make a clever, joking remark

repeal: To revoke, take back

repertoire: A set of well-rehearsed pieces for performance

replica: An exact copy

staple: Necessity

taint: To tarnish, spoil

thoroughfare: A wide, well-traveled street

wield: Carry in a menacing fashion

Picture Identifications

Cover: View of the Charles River with the Boston skyline, young Patriot reenactor playing a flute, Boston baked beans
Title Page: Necktie vendor at Faneuil Hall Marketplace
Pages 4–5: Boston Common and band shell
Pages 8–9: Boston artists doing caricatures
Pages 22–23: Painting of a Puritan family on the New England coast
Pages 32–33: Top-ranked runners starting the 101st Boston Marathon, 1997
Pages 42–43: Shoppers at Haymarket, a weekend open-air market on Blackstone Street
Page 43: Boston Baked Beans

Photo Credits ©:

NDEX

age numbers in boldface type indicate illustrations

TO FIND OUT MORE

BOOKS

Byers, Helen. *Kidding Around Boston: A Young Person's Guide to the City*. Santa Fe: John Muir Publications, 1997.

Dunnahoo, Terry. *Boston's Freedom Trail*. Places in American History series. Minneapolis: Dillon Press, 1995.

Fradin, Dennis B. *Massachusetts*. From Sea to Shining Sea series. Chicago: Childrens Press, 1991.

Fradin, Dennis B. *The Massachusetts Colony*. Chicago: Childrens Press, 1987.

Gibbons, Gail. *From Path to Highway: The Story of the Boston Post Road*. New York: Thomas Y. Crowell, 1986.

Goodman, Michael E. *Boston Celtics*. NBA Today series. Mankato, Minn.: Creative Education, 1998.

Kulper, Eileen. *The Boston Marathon*. Mankato, Minn.: Creative Education, 1993.

Kupelian, Vartan. *Boston Bruins*. Mankato, Minn.: Creative Education, 1996.

Moffat, Susan D. *Kids Explore Boston: The Very Best Kids' Activities within an Easy Drive of Boston*. Holbrook, Mass.: Adams Publishing, 1994.

Morris, Jerry. *The Boston Globe Guide to Boston*. 3rd edition. Old Saybrook, Conn.: The Globe Pequot Press, 1996.

Rambeck Richard. *Boston Red Sox*. Baseball the Great American Games series. Mankato, Minn.: Creative Education, 1992.

Stein, R. Conrad. *The Boston Tea Party*. Cornerstones of Freedom series. Chicago: Children's Press, 1996.

ONLINE SITES

4boston.com
http://www.4boston.com/
Links to everything in Boston: sports teams, museums, TV stations, restaurants, music, news, weather, and all those colleges!

Boston Celtics
http://www.nba.com/celtics
Meet the players, learn about the latest league (and Celtic) news, shop in the NBA store, order tickets. Plenty of stats, schedules, and scores.

Boston Globe
http://www.boston.com/globe
Find out what's happening in Boston, and the world. You're just a click away from sports, weather, columns, calendar of events, crossword puzzles, comics, and more.

Boston Marathon
http://www.baa.org/
The official website of Boston's most famous annual event. Find out who's running in the next marathon, and who's favored. Get the history and the latest news.

Faneuil Hall Marketplace
http://www.bostonian.com/faneuil/
Home to more than one hundred shops, restaurants, and special events, Faneuil Hall is one of Boston's most popular tourist attractions. Facts, photos, and history, too.

Harvard University
http://www.harvard.edu/
Maps, calendars, courses, museums, newsletters, pictures, student organizations, and much more. It's the easiest way to get into Harvard!

Museum of Fine Arts
http://www.mfa.org/home.html
See changing and ongoing exhibitions, learn what's coming up, visit the gift shop, or drop in on the museum's school.

Museum of Science
http://www.mos.org/
Visit online exhibits, find out about upcoming events, learn about the museum, and link to lots of other sites.

Museums
http://ftp.std.com/homepages/std/museums.html
This very useful site offers links to the best museums in the Boston area, as well as their addresses and telephone numbers. Includes the Boston Tea Party Museum, the Computer Museum, the Peabody, and plenty more.

ABOUT THE AUTHOR

Deborah Kent grew up in Little Falls, New Jersey, and received a B.A. in English from Oberlin College. She earned a master's degree from Smith College School of Social Work and worked for several years at the University Settlement House in New York City. For five years she lived in San Miguel de Allende, Mexico, where she wrote her first novel for young adults. Deborah Kent is the author of a dozen young-adult novels as well as many titles in the Childrens Press America the Beautiful series. She lives in Chicago with her husband and their daughter Janna.